Court Notes

Court Notes

Volleyball Journal

Richard Kent & David Gallagher

A companion book to

Writing on the Bus: Using Athletic Team Notebooks and Journals to Advance Learning and Performance in Sports

WritingAthletes.com

Dedications:

To Morgan and Caroline, my remarkable nieces… *RK*

To Mom and Dad, for your love and support on and off the court… *DG*

Acknowledgments:

Our thanks to Sheila Stawinski of the University of Vermont for her permission to modify and use her Performance Feedback form. We also thank Gayle Sirois for her editorial eye.

ISBN-13: 978-0-9860191-8-0

NATIONAL WRITING PROJECT

This book is published in cooperation with the National Writing Project, University of California, 2105 Bancroft Way, Berkeley, CA 94720

CONTENTS

WRITING YOUR GAME

For you as a player, keeping a volleyball journal is about learning and improving. Whether you're training at a volleyball camp, practicing on your own, or starting a new season with your team, writing in this journal can help you progress as an athlete by thinking about and analyzing your play.

It's pretty obvious that just writing about your training and match play isn't going to replace good coaching or dedicated training. You're not going to jump higher or score more points because you wrote a journal entry. But completing the activities in this journal will raise your volleyball IQ and make you a more knowledgeable volleyball player. With that knowledge you can improve on the court. That's exactly why Olympians and other elite athletes write in training logs, journals, and team notebooks.

Before each section of this journal, you'll find instructions and in some cases a model. Here are the sections of your journal:

Journal Prompts: forty-eight (48) journal prompts to help you think about your game and yourself. If a particular prompt doesn't work for you, cross it out and write what's uppermost in your mind.

Additional Journal Pages: seven (7) extra pages when you have more to say about a particular journal prompt.

Match Analyses I: sixteen (16) analysis pages that will guide you in analyzing a match your team played in. Even if you sat the bench, analyze the match. This experience is about learning and knowing the game.

Performance Feedback: five (5) pages that will help you think about the stressors you face before, during, and after a match.

Match Analyses II: four (4) analysis pages that will guide you in unpacking a match you watched in person, on video, or online.

Notes Pages: five (5) blank pages and five volleyball court diagrams to use for notes, drawings, team formations, and more.

We want to emphasize that this is your journal. Write what's true for you as a player and person. Address your weaknesses—don't avoid them—and focus on improvement.

We challenge you to think deeply, to explore your understanding of volleyball, and to see yourself at the next level. Visualize your best—then plan and practice to get there. We know writing can help.

VOLLEYBALL JOURNAL PROMPTS

Instructions for Writing Journals

Your journal includes 48 prompts. Many of these prompts can be composed in 3-5 minutes; they're called Quick Write Journals. When you begin a journal entry, try not to stop; keep your pen or pencil on the paper and keep writing. Be inventive and keep moving!

If your mind goes blank while you're writing a journal entry, make a list of words related to the topic. When your ideas begin to flow, start writing sentences again. If you run out of space and have more to say, continue writing on the additional blank journal pages provided starting on page 59. And when you're writing, please don't be too concerned with the conventions of writing, e.g., spelling, grammar, or paragraphing. Just write.

1.

What are your strengths as a volleyball player right now? When asked to name a strength, some players said that they were…

Focused	Dedicated	Fit	Inventive
Confident	Competitive	Motivated	Brave
Responsible	Positive	Skillful	Strong

List some of your strengths here:

Now write about your primary strength as a player…

2.

Think about an aspect of volleyball that you'd like to improve upon. Maybe you'd like to be a better passer or create more innovative offensive plays. Search YouTube or other websites for a video on what you want you'd like to focus on. Watch the video and write about what you observe:

Skill: _______________ Title of Video: ______________________________

–What new information did you learn?

–What might you try out or how might you adapt your play?

–What questions did you have after watching the video?

–What ideas might you share with a fellow player?

–What knowledge might you share with your coach?

–What other search terms might you use to find other videos in the future:

3.

Mental Imagery: Think back and recall your best moments as a player. Remember the exact details of a perfect dig, brilliant backset, or powerful line shot. Make a list of those moments and create your own mental performance video that you can play back to yourself in preparation for a game, or to use during a competition to gain back confidence. Your mental performance video might last between 10-30 seconds.

Image:

Image:

Image:

Image:

Image:

4.

Write about one of your favorite teammates or training partners.

Name or initials: ______________________

Qualities as an athlete:

Qualities as a person:

Unique habits or quirks:

A story you'd share about this athlete:

What have you learned from this athlete?

More:

5.

Write about your strengths and/or challenges with the following:

Underhand Passing:

Overhand Passing:

Blocking:

Serving:

Hitting:

Digging:

Back-row Attacking:

Setting:

Defensive Transitioning:

Of the skills listed which two do you really need to work on? Explain:

6.

Who brings out the best in you as a volleyball player and why? You might first think of a coach, manager, or trainer. But also think about family members, friends, fans, teammates, or even an opponent.

7.

What makes training hard for you?

What makes training easy for you?

8.

What foods will help me play my best during a long match. . .

During a volleyball match I am nervous about . . .

My favorite exercise or activity during a training session is . . .

When I hear ______________________________ from an opponent or an opponent's fan, I feel like . . .

When my team wins a match by a wide margin, I . . .

When my coach says _____________________ I feel like . . .

9.

Outline what you consider a perfect warm-up routine for a training session. Make a list of each activity on the left; then include the approximate amount of time spent on the activity and offer a reason you have included it.

Warm-up Activities	How long?	Why this activity?

10.

Make a list of your favorite "things" in volleyball. They could be plays, moments, equipment, places, or people. Here's an example: the moment after a close tiebreaker set.

11.

Write a letter to one of your former coaches. You may wish to include: what you're doing now as a player; the coach's contributions to your life; the issues you currently face as a player; a fun memory; a photo. You may wish to mail or email a revised version of the letter to your former coach.

12.

"Some days, playing poorly is the most important result that could happen." Give an example from your own experience as an athlete why this statement can be true.

13.

How do you learn volleyball? Look at this figure and circle the ways you learn as a player.

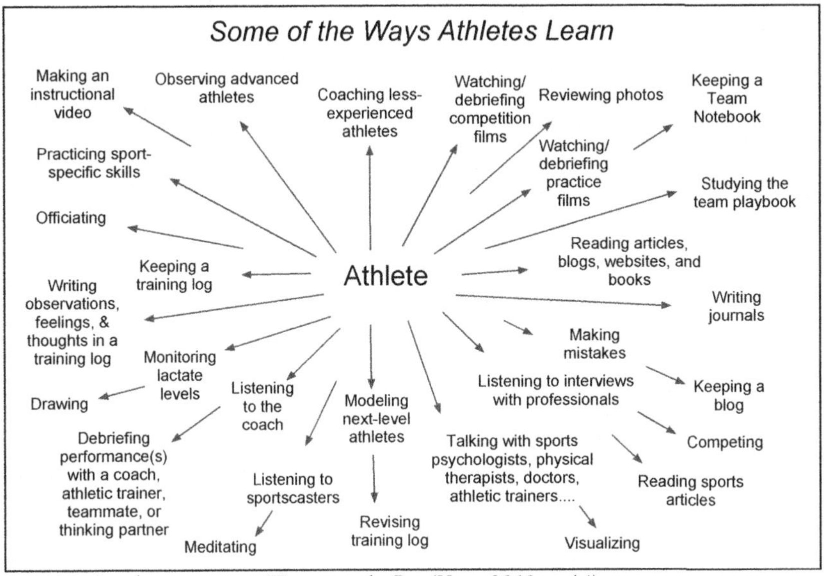

Reprinted with permission, *Writing on the Bus* (Kent, 2012, p. 14)

From the various learning activities above that you did not circle, which ones could you add to your experience to help you improve as a player? Explain.

List any ways that you learn volleyball that are not included in the figure above.

14.

Describe your most humiliating experience as an athlete. What might you have learned from this experience?

15.

In this journal entry, you're going to create a volleyball playlist.

Make a list of your favorite songs down the left side:

Which of those favorite songs would you play…

The night before an important match:

Song title: ____________________

During training:

Song title: ____________________

The morning of a match:

Song title: ____________________

During a match:

Song title: ____________________

After an upset win:

Song title: ____________________

After a loss to an opponent you could have beaten:

Song title: ____________________

When the season ends:

Song title: ____________________

Others times: ________________

Song title: ____________________

Others times: ________________

Song title: ____________________

16.

Using your most recent competition, respond to the following:

–Describe the evening before this competition. Did you prepare the way you should have?

–On game day, how did you spend your time? Did you eat/hydrate adequately? If you could improve one aspect of your preparation for this competition, what would it be?

–Describe your pre-game preparation (e.g., warm-up). Is there any aspect of your pre-game that you'd improve upon?

–Describe your mindset during the competition. Were you focused and motivated?

–Describe your post-game recovery. Did you stretch, hydrate, and eat appropriately? Is there any aspect of your post-game that you'd change?

17.

Describe your earliest memories as a volleyball player.

18.

Make a list of five qualities you believe an effective coach must have. Give an example from a coach you know.

Quality ________________________________:

Quality ________________________________:

Quality ________________________________:

Quality ________________________________:

Quality ________________________________:

19.

Think about the role of volleyball coaches and officials. Maybe you've done some coaching or officiating in volleyball. Maybe not. Whatever your experience, write about the following prompts:

–What are the most challenging aspects of being a volleyball coach?

–What are some of the most challenging aspects of being a volleyball official?

–As a player, is there anything you could do to assist coaches or officials with their jobs?

20.

Describe the last time you lost your cool in a match. How did it affect your play? Did anyone say anything to you? What did you learn from this experience?

21.

If you could relive one moment as a volleyball player, what would it be and why would you want to go back?

22.

Think of a volleyball player that you respect. What do you admire about this player?

23.

Think back to when you were a young athlete. What would you say as that young person about the athlete you've become?

24.

What is something you dislike about yourself as an athlete? Write about how you confront or work on this issue in an effort to improve.

25.

Think back through your athletic career and make a list of the teams you've played on or the age levels you competed at. What did you learn at each level? Who do you remember from those days? You can also include experiences like pick-up games with friends.

Example:
Team/Age Group *My Town Middle School Volleyball Team*:

I knew nothing about volleyball when I signed up for the team. My best friend played so I wanted to. I learned how to cover the hitter and how to hit an angle shot. If it wasn't for my coach, I'm not sure I would have continued playing when going to high school.

Team/Age Group____________________:

Team/Age Group____________________:

Team/Age Group____________________:

Team/Age Group____________________:

Team/Age Group____________________:

26.

In volleyball, there are things we can control and things we can't. For example, we can't control a referee's call, our coach's decisions, or what someone says about us. We can control the amount of sleep we get, the volume and quality of training we do, the diet we maintain, and the attitude we bring to a practice or match. Write about a time when you let something you could not control get the better of you. What happened? How did you react? What would you do now under the same circumstances?

27.

How do you prepare for a match? Many players have routines that they follow. They may go to bed at a certain time, eat specific foods, listen to particular music, or talk with certain people. Some players review their own "game plans" and, using mental imagery, "watch" their mental performance video like you created in Journal #3 on page 13. Write about your pre-match routines. If you have not established one or wish to revise the one you have, write about that.

28.

Make a list of five good things that are happening in your life right now outside of sport. Select one or two and write about them.

1. ____

2. ____

3. ____

4. ____

5. ____

29.

It's often said that we are who we spend the most time with. Who are the three people, athletes or not, that you spend the most time with? In what ways do they influence who you are?

30.

Make a list of what you say to yourself during a volleyball game. You may well want to write down this "self-talk" just after a game. This internal dialog may include feelings ("We're going to destroy this team."), instructions you give yourself ("Hang back! Delay! Move your feet!"), or random thoughts ("What did that fan just say to Alex?")

31.

Read through your list of self-talk on the previous page and write about what you notice. Is your talk positive, instructive, and motivating? Do you spend too much time complaining about a teammate, the coach, or an official? Is your self-talk productive or destructive, positive or negative, informative or unhelpful?

32.

Make a list of 10 favorite quotations by volleyball players or athletes from other sports. You may find lists of quotations by athletes by searching the internet.

33.

What's the best volleyball match (or other competition) that you've seen in person? Describe the details and explain what made it *the best.*

34.

Make a list of people—athletes or not—that you would stand in a very long line to meet. What do these people have in common? In your eyes, what does this list say about you?

35.

What is your favorite place to compete and why?

36.

Throughout your time as a player, you may have discovered some favorite resources that you've used to expand your knowledge and enjoyment of volleyball. Make a list of the websites, YouTube videos, books, magazines, Facebook pages, or movies that you would recommend to a younger player. If you don't have many, ask friends or teammates for their favorites.

37.

What is a good opponent?

38.

Watch a game on television, online, or a video. Make a list of some the announcer's best descriptive lines. What's your favorite and why?

39.

Under each category below, name a teammate, volleyball camp friend, or even an opponent. Give an example or two of the athlete's qualities.

Tag a VB Teammate

Who'd make a great coach?	A true sportsman	Dedication plus	Kindest
Most coachable	Always leaves it on the court	Most motivating	Great future
Great opponent	Team Leader	Fun	Positive
Healthy	Student-Athlete: the complete package	Who should take the last hit?	Fitness Fanatic

40.

A class of sports psychology students explored how failure can be helpful. Among the list compiled by students were the following—write about them:

Failure found what didn't work.

Failure creates hunger to do better.

Failure adds value to success.

Failure is feedback.

41.

What advice or talk do you least like to hear before an important game? Why?

42.

Come up with four T-shirt slogans/sayings about your team, volleyball, competing, or training. Use the t-shirts provided. To jumpstart your thinking, here's a popular team slogan: *Teamwork makes the dream work.*

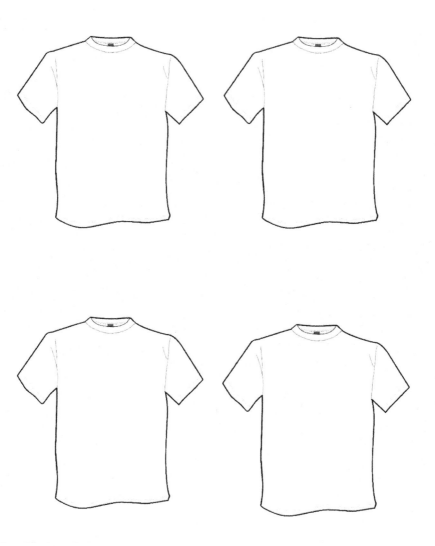

43.

Write about this quotation:

"Adversity, if you allow it to, will fortify you and make you the best you can be." –Kerri Walsh Jennings, 3x Olympic Gold Medalist

44.

Draw a picture of your favorite piece of sports equipment and write one sentence about it.

45.

Write about the kindest thing you have ever done as an athlete.

46.

Throughout your volleyball season or camp, you experience highs and lows, ups and down. Think back and give quick examples of the following:

I laughed…

I got emotional or cried…

I screamed like a wild person…

I became crazy angry…

I sat and stared in disbelief…

I just didn't care…

I wanted to go hide…

I wanted someone to see…

47.

We are our thoughts and actions. In the callout bubble below, list the <u>individual</u> words (not phrases or sentences) that you believe represent you as both an athlete and person.

48.

> "Writing organizes and clarifies our thoughts. Writing is how we think our way into a subject and make it our own. Writing enables us to find out what we know—and what we don't know—about whatever we're trying to learn." –William Zinsser

In what ways has this quotation proven true for you as an athlete who has kept a journal?

ADDITIONAL JOURNALING PAGES

Journal #_____

Journal #_____

Journal #_____

Journal #_____

Journal #_____

Journal #_____

Journal #_____

MATCH ANALYSIS I

Instructions for *Match Analysis I*

The prompts on these pages provide you with an opportunity to analyze your match. Unpacking a volleyball match in this fashion, whether you were a reserve or played every minute, helps you think more objectively while seeing the larger picture of a game. This thinking will help you improve your understanding of volleyball. The *MAI* may be used for practice games and intrasquad contests as well as your league or conference games.

When you fill out an *MAI*, don't be overly concerned about the conventions of writing. In other words, don't worry about spelling, grammar, and paragraphing… *just write.*

Check out the model *MAI* on the next page and look closely at the way the player addressed certain prompts. But remember, these are just models—you'll have your own way of telling the story of a match.

In the final section of the *MAI*, you'll see a Player Check-in. This section can usually be accomplished quickly. Don't sit around and ponder life. Give a general response that reflects your immediate thought. Rate each topic in the Player Check-in using the following scale:

Above Average (+)   Average (O)   Below Average (–)

As you go through these topics, focus on the following:

Health: How's my over all health?

Sleep: Am I getting enough sleep each night?

Hydration: Do I take in enough water throughout the day as well as before, during, and after a match?

Fitness: How's my overall fitness level?

Nutrition: The USDA has a basic informational website that offers nutritional guidance about the consumption of food (see ChooseMyPlate.Gov). For purposes of the Player Check-in, ask yourself whether you've eaten the suggested foods of a healthy diet, including grains, proteins, veggies, and fruit.

–MODEL–

Match Analysis I

Opponent: *Bryan HS* (W *3* L 1) *Date: 9/18* Result: *1-0 W* Court: *Home*
Record: Wins: 4 Losses: 0

- My strengths as a player in today's match:
  I rotated well on defense and made sure to cover the hitters—even saving two blocked balls ☺ I had very few hitting errors.

- My weaknesses as a player in today's match:
  I could have been more supportive of Jason. When I encourage him he plays better.

- Team strengths in today's match:
  We worked as a team—great support—positive comments… Good adjustments after the first game.

- Team weaknesses in today's match:
  We relied on our left sides too much; didn't utilize the middle attack to mix things up.

- Opponent's strengths:
  LHS never let down. #9 dug everything. He chased down just about every ball.

- Opponent's weaknesses:
  They had difficulty passing when we served deep and to the corners.

- What was the "difference" in today's match:
  Their blockers couldn't stop our outside attack. Matt couldn't be stopped.

- What team adjustment would you suggest for the next match against this opponent?

  Use the middle more to further free up our outside attack.

- Who was the Player of the Match and why?
  Ryan's consistent hitting outside, with very few unforced errors, was the difference for us.

- Other comments (e.g., team strategy, attitude, preparation….)
  We were prepared! The seniors had us ready to play. Un-DE-feated!

Player Check-in

Above Average (+) Average (O) Below Average (–)

Health	+	*Nutrition:*	Grains	O
Sleep	O		Protein	+
Hydration	O		Veggies	–
Fitness	+		Fruit	O

Life Beyond Volleyball O

Quotable Quote:

"The guy's not human!" by Dusty about #9 BHS

Match Analysis I

Opponent: ___________ (W__ L__) Date: ____ Result: _____ Court: ____
Record: Wins: ___ Losses: ___

- My strengths as a player in today's match:

- My weaknesses as a player in today's match:

- Team strengths in today's match:

- Team weaknesses in today's match:

- Opponent's strengths:

- Opponent's weaknesses:

- What was the "difference" in today's match:

- What team adjustment would you suggest for the next match against this opponent?

- Who was the Player of the Match and why?

- Other comments (e.g., team strategy, attitude, preparation....)

Player Check-in

Above Average (+) Average (O) Below Average (–)

Health	___	*Nutrition:*	Grains	___
Sleep	___		Protein	___
Hydration	___		Veggies	___
Fitness	___		Fruit	___

Life Beyond Volleyball ___

Quotable Quote:

Match Analysis I

Opponent: ___________ (W__ L__) Date: ____ Result: ____ Court: ____
Record: Wins: ___ Losses: ___

- My strengths as a player in today's match:

- My weaknesses as a player in today's match:

- Team strengths in today's match:

- Team weaknesses in today's match:

- Opponent's strengths:

- Opponent's weaknesses:

- What was the "difference" in today's match:

- What team adjustment would you suggest for the next match against this opponent?

- Who was the Player of the Match and why?

- Other comments (e.g., team strategy, attitude, preparation….)

Player Check-in

Above Average (+) Average (O) Below Average (–)

Health	___	*Nutrition:*	Grains	___
Sleep	___		Protein	___
Hydration	___		Veggies	___
Fitness	___		Fruit	___

Life Beyond Volleyball ___

Quotable Quote:

____

____

Match Analysis I

Opponent: __________ (W__ L__) Date: ____ Result: ____ Court: ____
Record: Wins: ___ Losses: ___

- My strengths as a player in today's match:

- My weaknesses as a player in today's match:

- Team strengths in today's match:

- Team weaknesses in today's match:

- Opponent's strengths:

- Opponent's weaknesses:

- What was the "difference" in today's match:

- What team adjustment would you suggest for the next match against this opponent?

- Who was the Player of the Match and why?

- Other comments (e.g., team strategy, attitude, preparation….)

Player Check-in

Above Average (+) Average (O) Below Average (–)

Health	___	*Nutrition:*	Grains	___
Sleep	___		Protein	___
Hydration	___		Veggies	___
Fitness	___		Fruit	___

Life Beyond Volleyball ___

Quotable Quote:

Match Analysis I

Opponent: ___________ (W__ L__) Date: ____ Result: ____ Court: ____
Record: Wins: ___ Losses: ___

- My strengths as a player in today's match:

- My weaknesses as a player in today's match:

- Team strengths in today's match:

- Team weaknesses in today's match:

- Opponent's strengths:

- Opponent's weaknesses:

- What was the "difference" in today's match:

- What team adjustment would you suggest for the next match against this opponent?

- Who was the Player of the Match and why?

- Other comments (e.g., team strategy, attitude, preparation....)

Player Check-in

Above Average (+) Average (O) Below Average (–)

Health	___	*Nutrition:*	Grains	___
Sleep	___		Protein	___
Hydration	___		Veggies	___
Fitness	___		Fruit	___

Life Beyond Volleyball ___

Quotable Quote:

____

____

Match Analysis I

Opponent: __________ (W__ L__) Date: ____ Result: ____ Court: ____
Record: Wins: ___ Losses: ___

- My strengths as a player in today's match:

- My weaknesses as a player in today's match:

- Team strengths in today's match:

- Team weaknesses in today's match:

- Opponent's strengths:

- Opponent's weaknesses:

- What was the "difference" in today's match:

- What team adjustment would you suggest for the next match against this opponent?

- Who was the Player of the Match and why?

- Other comments (e.g., team strategy, attitude, preparation….)

Player Check-in

Above Average (+) Average (O) Below Average (–)

Health	___	*Nutrition:*	Grains	___
Sleep	___		Protein	___
Hydration	___		Veggies	___
Fitness	___		Fruit	___

Life Beyond Volleyball ___

Quotable Quote:

___

___

Match Analysis I

Opponent: __________ (W__ L__) Date: ____ Result: ____ Court: ____
Record: Wins: ___ Losses: ___

- My strengths as a player in today's match:

- My weaknesses as a player in today's match:

- Team strengths in today's match:

- Team weaknesses in today's match:

- Opponent's strengths:

- Opponent's weaknesses:

- What was the “difference” in today’s match:

- What team adjustment would you suggest for the next match against this opponent?

- Who was the Player of the Match and why?

- Other comments (e.g., team strategy, attitude, preparation….)

Player Check-in

Above Average (+) Average (O) Below Average (–)

Health	___	*Nutrition:*	Grains	___
Sleep	___		Protein	___
Hydration	___		Veggies	___
Fitness	___		Fruit	___

Life Beyond Volleyball ___

Quotable Quote:

Match Analysis I

Opponent: __________ (W__ L__) Date: ____ Result: ____ Court: ____
Record: Wins: ___ Losses: ___

- My strengths as a player in today's match:

- My weaknesses as a player in today's match:

- Team strengths in today's match:

- Team weaknesses in today's match:

- Opponent's strengths:

- Opponent's weaknesses:

- What was the "difference" in today's match:

- What team adjustment would you suggest for the next match against this opponent?

- Who was the Player of the Match and why?

- Other comments (e.g., team strategy, attitude, preparation….)

Player Check-in

Above Average (+) Average (O) Below Average (–)

Health	___	*Nutrition:*	Grains	___
Sleep	___		Protein	___
Hydration	___		Veggies	___
Fitness	___		Fruit	___

Life Beyond Volleyball ___

Quotable Quote:

____

____

Match Analysis I

Opponent: ___________ (W__ L__) Date: ____ Result: ____ Court: ____
Record: Wins: ___ Losses: ___

- My strengths as a player in today's match:

- My weaknesses as a player in today's match:

- Team strengths in today's match:

- Team weaknesses in today's match:

- Opponent's strengths:

- Opponent's weaknesses:

- What was the "difference" in today's match:

- What team adjustment would you suggest for the next match against this opponent?

- Who was the Player of the Match and why?

- Other comments (e.g., team strategy, attitude, preparation….)

Player Check-in

Above Average (+) Average (O) Below Average (–)

Health	___	*Nutrition:*	Grains	___
Sleep	___		Protein	___
Hydration	___		Veggies	___
Fitness	___		Fruit	___

Life Beyond Volleyball ___

Quotable Quote:

___

___

Match Analysis I

Opponent: __________ (W__ L__) Date: ____ Result: ____ Court: ____
Record: Wins: ___ Losses: ___

- My strengths as a player in today's match:

- My weaknesses as a player in today's match:

- Team strengths in today's match:

- Team weaknesses in today's match:

- Opponent's strengths:

- Opponent's weaknesses:

- What was the "difference" in today's match:

- What team adjustment would you suggest for the next match against this opponent?

- Who was the Player of the Match and why?

- Other comments (e.g., team strategy, attitude, preparation….)

Player Check-in

Above Average (+) Average (O) Below Average (–)

Health	___	*Nutrition:*	Grains	___
Sleep	___		Protein	___
Hydration	___		Veggies	___
Fitness	___		Fruit	___

Life Beyond Volleyball ___

Quotable Quote:

____

____

Match Analysis I

Opponent: ___________ (W__ L__) Date: ____ Result: ____ Court: ____
Record: Wins: ___ Losses: ___

- My strengths as a player in today's match:

- My weaknesses as a player in today's match:

- Team strengths in today's match:

- Team weaknesses in today's match:

- Opponent's strengths:

- Opponent's weaknesses:

- What was the "difference" in today's match:

- What team adjustment would you suggest for the next match against this opponent?

- Who was the Player of the Match and why?

- Other comments (e.g., team strategy, attitude, preparation….)

Player Check-in

Above Average (+) Average (O) Below Average (–)

Health	___	*Nutrition:*	Grains	___
Sleep	___		Protein	___
Hydration	___		Veggies	___
Fitness	___		Fruit	___

Life Beyond Volleyball ___

Quotable Quote:

Match Analysis I

Opponent: __________ (W__ L__) Date: ____ Result: ____ Court: ____
Record: Wins: ___ Losses: ___

- My strengths as a player in today's match:

- My weaknesses as a player in today's match:

- Team strengths in today's match:

- Team weaknesses in today's match:

- Opponent's strengths:

- Opponent's weaknesses:

- What was the "difference" in today's match:

- What team adjustment would you suggest for the next match against this opponent?

- Who was the Player of the Match and why?

- Other comments (e.g., team strategy, attitude, preparation….)

Player Check-in

Above Average (+) Average (O) Below Average (–)

Health	___	*Nutrition:*	Grains	___
Sleep	___		Protein	___
Hydration	___		Veggies	___
Fitness	___		Fruit	___

Life Beyond Volleyball ___

Quotable Quote:

____

____

Match Analysis I

Opponent: __________ (W__ L__) Date: ____ Result: ____ Court: ____
Record: Wins: ___ Losses: ___

- My strengths as a player in today's match:

- My weaknesses as a player in today's match:

- Team strengths in today's match:

- Team weaknesses in today's match:

- Opponent's strengths:

- Opponent's weaknesses:

- What was the "difference" in today's match:

- What team adjustment would you suggest for the next match against this opponent?

- Who was the Player of the Match and why?

- Other comments (e.g., team strategy, attitude, preparation….)

Player Check-in

Above Average (+) Average (O) Below Average (–)

Health	___	*Nutrition:*	Grains	___
Sleep	___		Protein	___
Hydration	___		Veggies	___
Fitness	___		Fruit	___

Life Beyond Volleyball ___

Quotable Quote:

____

____

Match Analysis I

Opponent: __________ (W__ L__) Date: ____ Result: ____ Court: ____
Record: Wins: ___ Losses: ___

- My strengths as a player in today's match:

- My weaknesses as a player in today's match:

- Team strengths in today's match:

- Team weaknesses in today's match:

- Opponent's strengths:

- Opponent's weaknesses:

- What was the "difference" in today's match:

- What team adjustment would you suggest for the next match against this opponent?

- Who was the Player of the Match and why?

- Other comments (e.g., team strategy, attitude, preparation….)

Player Check-in

Above Average (+) Average (O) Below Average (–)

Health	___	*Nutrition:*	Grains	___
Sleep	___		Protein	___
Hydration	___		Veggies	___
Fitness	___		Fruit	___

Life Beyond Volleyball ___

Quotable Quote:

Match Analysis I

Opponent: ___________ (W__ L__) Date: ____ Result: ____ Court: ____
Record: Wins: ___ Losses: ___

- My strengths as a player in today's match:

- My weaknesses as a player in today's match:

- Team strengths in today's match:

- Team weaknesses in today's match:

- Opponent's strengths:

- Opponent's weaknesses:

- What was the "difference" in today's match:

- What team adjustment would you suggest for the next match against this opponent?

- Who was the Player of the Match and why?

- Other comments (e.g., team strategy, attitude, preparation….)

Player Check-in

Above Average (+) Average (O) Below Average (–)

Health	___	*Nutrition:*	Grains	___
Sleep	___		Protein	___
Hydration	___		Veggies	___
Fitness	___		Fruit	___

Life Beyond Volleyball ___

Quotable Quote:

Match Analysis I

Opponent: ___________ (W__ L__) Date: ____ Result: ____ Court: ____
Record: Wins: ___ Losses: ___

- My strengths as a player in today's match:

- My weaknesses as a player in today's match:

- Team strengths in today's match:

- Team weaknesses in today's match:

- Opponent's strengths:

- Opponent's weaknesses:

- What was the "difference" in today's match:

- What team adjustment would you suggest for the next match against this opponent?

- Who was the Player of the Match and why?

- Other comments (e.g., team strategy, attitude, preparation….)

Player Check-in

Above Average (+) Average (O) Below Average (–)

Health	___	*Nutrition:*	Grains	___
Sleep	___		Protein	___
Hydration	___		Veggies	___
Fitness	___		Fruit	___

Life Beyond Volleyball ___

Quotable Quote:

Match Analysis I

Opponent: __________ (W__ L__) Date: ____ Result: ____ Court: ____
Record: Wins: ___ Losses: ___

- My strengths as a player in today's match:

- My weaknesses as a player in today's match:

- Team strengths in today's match:

- Team weaknesses in today's match:

- Opponent's strengths:

- Opponent's weaknesses:

- What was the "difference" in today's match:

- What team adjustment would you suggest for the next match against this opponent?

- Who was the Player of the Match and why?

- Other comments (e.g., team strategy, attitude, preparation….)

Player Check-in

Above Average (+) Average (O) Below Average (–)

Health	___	*Nutrition:*	Grains	___
Sleep	___		Protein	___
Hydration	___		Veggies	___
Fitness	___		Fruit	___

Life Beyond Volleyball ___

Quotable Quote:

PERFORMANCE FEEDBACK

INSTRUCTIONS FOR PERFORMANCE FEEDBACK

At different times throughout your volleyball season, camp, or tour, fill out one of the following Performance Feedback forms immediately after a match. This form helps you look closely at the stress you experience before and during a game. As an athlete, writing about stressors can help you manage those feelings in the future.

–MODEL–

Performance Feedback

Opponent: UNB   Date: September 18

What stressors did you experience before, during, and after this match?

At the last practice coach told me that I should be ready to set if we get a big lead. I haven't had many chances to set, so I was nervous all day before the match.

How did you experience this stress? Did it manifest in your thoughts, in the way you felt, or in the way you acted?

I found myself getting more nervous after we won the first game. When I got the chance to get out there and set, my nerves disappeared. I was just trying to run the offense and get the ball where it needed to go.

Mark on this scale your level of excitement and motivation for the match.

0---------------------------------------5--------X---------------------------------10

Too Low   Perfect   Too High

In a few words, describe your feelings at the various times in the day?

Travel to match: *Really nervous*
Warm up: *Excited*
Just before the match: *Relaxed*
During the match: *Nervous, then ready to play*
After the match: *Super excited that I got the chance to set*

What techniques did you use to manage any stress you experienced? How effective were you in controlling this stress?

I talked to my teammates in order to keep my mind off of it, and just went through my typical warm-up. This seemed to work during warm-up, but then as we sat on the bench my nerves started to get the best of me.

How was your self-talk? Positive, negative, thoughtful?

I kept telling myself that I have wanted to set for the team all season and that this was my chance. After we won our second game and coach said to get ready, I tried to act like this wasn't a big deal. I just kept saying, "This isn't a big deal, I can do this."

Describe how your stressors, excitement/motivation, and self-talk impacted your performance.

I think my stress and excitement leading up to the match was a little much. I couldn't focus on anything but the game. During the match, my self-talk helped me focus on what I was to do when out on the court. Overall, I was able to manage the stress and excitement, not letting it overwhelm me too much.

After unpacking your game-day mental state, what would you do differently to improve for the next match?

I think I would try my self-talk earlier in the day. I could also maybe try to distract myself with hanging out with my friends before the game.

What's one thing you learned from completing this Performance Feedback form?

Before completing this form, I'm not sure I really thought that I could do much about my nerves. Maybe I can ask my friends what they do to manage stress.

Performance Feedback

Opponent: __________ Date: ____________

What stressors did you experience before, during, and after this match?

How did you experience this stress? Did it manifest in your thoughts, in the way you felt, or in the way you acted?

Mark on this scale your level of excitement and motivation for the match.

0--5--10

Too Low Perfect Too High

In a few words, describe your feelings at the various times in the day?

Travel to match:
Warm up:
Just before the match:
During the match:
After the match:

What techniques did you use to manage any stress you experienced? How effective were you in controlling this stress?

How was your self-talk? Positive, negative, thoughtful?

Describe how your stressors, excitement/motivation, and self-talk impacted your performance.

After unpacking your game-day mental state, what would you do differently to improve for the next match?

What's one thing you learned from completing this Performance Feedback form?

Performance Feedback

Opponent: ___________ Date: _____________

What stressors did you experience before, during, and after this match?

How did you experience this stress? Did it manifest in your thoughts, in the way you felt, or in the way you acted?

Mark on this scale your level of excitement and motivation for the match.

0--------------------------------------5---10

Too Low Perfect Too High

In a few words, describe your feelings at the various times in the day?

Travel to match:
Warm up:
Just before the match:
During the match:
After the match:

What techniques did you use to manage any stress you experienced? How effective were you in controlling this stress?

How was your self-talk? Positive, negative, thoughtful?

Describe how your stressors, excitement/motivation, and self-talk impacted your performance.

After unpacking your game-day mental state, what would you do differently to improve for the next match?

What's one thing you learned from completing this Performance Feedback form?

Performance Feedback

Opponent: __________ Date: ____________

What stressors did you experience before, during, and after this match?

How did you experience this stress? Did it manifest in your thoughts, in the way you felt, or in the way you acted?

Mark on this scale your level of excitement and motivation for the match.

0--5--10

Too Low   Perfect   Too High

In a few words, describe your feelings at the various times in the day?

Travel to match:
Warm up:
Just before the match:
During the match:
After the match:

What techniques did you use to manage any stress you experienced? How effective were you in controlling this stress?

How was your self-talk? Positive, negative, thoughtful?

Describe how your stressors, excitement/motivation, and self-talk impacted your performance.

After unpacking your game-day mental state, what would you do differently to improve for the next match?

What's one thing you learned from completing this Performance Feedback form?

Performance Feedback

Opponent: __________ Date: ____________

What stressors did you experience before, during, and after this match?

How did you experience this stress? Did it manifest in your thoughts, in the way you felt, or in the way you acted?

Mark on this scale your level of excitement and motivation for the match.

0--5--10

Too Low Perfect Too High

In a few words, describe your feelings at the various times in the day?

Travel to match:
Warm up:
Just before the match:
During the match:
After the match:

What techniques did you use to manage any stress you experienced? How effective were you in controlling this stress?

How was your self-talk? Positive, negative, thoughtful?

Describe how your stressors, excitement/motivation, and self-talk impacted your performance.

After unpacking your game-day mental state, what would you do differently to improve for the next match?

What's one thing you learned from completing this Performance Feedback form?

Performance Feedback

Opponent: ___________ Date: ______________

What stressors did you experience before, during, and after this match?

How did you experience this stress? Did it manifest in your thoughts, in the way you felt, or in the way you acted?

Mark on this scale your level of excitement and motivation for the match.

0--5--10

Too Low Perfect Too High

In a few words, describe your feelings at the various times in the day?

Travel to match:
Warm up:
Just before the match:
During the match:
After the match:

What techniques did you use to manage any stress you experienced? How effective were you in controlling this stress?

How was your self-talk? Positive, negative, thoughtful?

Describe how your stressors, excitement/motivation, and self-talk impacted your performance.

After unpacking your game-day mental state, what would you do differently to improve for the next match?

What's one thing you learned from completing this Performance Feedback form?

MATCH ANALYSIS II

INSTRUCTIONS FOR MATCH ANALYSIS II

Throughout the year, you'll have opportunities to analyze matches that you've watched in person, on TV, or online. Filling out the Match Analysis II can help you look more objectively at those games. A learning activity, the *MAII* challenges you to watch a match more critically, more fully, and more like a coach than an athlete. Unpacking a volleyball match with the Match Analysis II will guide you to becoming a more thoughtful *student of the game.*

Review the model Match Analysis II on the following couple of pages.

—MODEL—

Match Analysis II

Team #1 Torrence HS
Wins: *6* Losses: *4*
Date: *September 29*

Offense/Rotation:
6-2

Strengths:
Outside hitters were consistent.
Setter got the ball to outsides no matter where the pass went.

Weaknesses:
They seemed to relax when they were up 2-0.

Team #2 Freedom HS
Wins: *7* Losses: *3*
Court: *Hosmer*

Offense/Rotation:
5-1

Strengths:
Middle blockers
Resilient team

Weaknesses:
Didn't pass well.
Lots of hitting errors.

In-game Adjustments & Effects

None. They thought they were going to cruise to win.
Over confident.

Hid some of their passers.
Better passing led to more opportunities for hitters.

General Comments

Left Sides
Consistent

Right Side(s)/Opposite
Made mistakes late in match.

Setter(s)
Were really good.

Middles
Moved well.

Left Sides
Hit well when set was there.

Right Side(s)/Opposite
Consistent—few mistakes.

Setter(s)
Lost composure—
Able to get it back when passing improved.

Middles
Got their hands on everything.

Libero

Confident—great technique—
Team leader.

Libero

Poor positioning.
No talk after second game.

Player(s) of the Match

#6—Libero. She got to everything.
She always was encouraging the team.
She's the kind of player I'd like to be.

Middle—she kept her cool.
It's not easy leading young
players.

Moment of the Match

#6 running down the ball to save the point and keep the lead in the fourth game. She gets to everything! !Phenomenal!

Final Analysis

FHS needed to work on the simple things: passing and ball control with their outsides. They were a lot younger than THS and just needed to try to play within themselves. It's like you told us over the last two years. Play the fundamentals—it's a simple game so keep it that way. As for THS, they didn't stay focused for the whole match. They thought they were going to cruise to victory; need to know when to finish a team.

Match Analysis II

Team #1__________________ Team #2____________________

Wins: ___ Losses: ___ Wins: ___ Losses: ___

Date: _____________________ Court: ______________________

Offense/Rotation:

Strengths:

Weaknesses:

Offense/Rotation:

Strengths:

Weaknesses:

In-game Adjustments & Effects

General Comments

Left Sides

Right Side(s)/Opposite

Setter(s)

Middles

Libero

Left Sides

Right Side(s)/Opposite

Setter(s)

Middles

Libero

Player(s) of the Match

Moment of the Match

Final Analysis

Notes

Match Analysis II

Team #1__________________ Team #2____________________

Wins: ___ Losses: ___ Wins: ___ Losses: ___

Date: ______________________ Court: _______________________

Offense/Rotation:

Strengths:

Weaknesses:

Offense/Rotation:

Strengths:

Weaknesses:

In-game Adjustments & Effects

General Comments

Left Sides

Right Side(s)/Opposite

Setter(s)

Middles

Libero

Left Sides

Right Side(s)/Opposite

Setter(s)

Middles

Libero

Player(s) of the Match

Moment of the Match

Final Analysis

Notes

Match Analysis II

Team #1___________________	Team #2_____________________
Wins: ___ Losses: ___	Wins: ___ Losses: ___
Date: ________________________	Court: _________________________
Offense/Rotation:	Offense/Rotation:
Strengths:	Strengths:
Weaknesses:	Weaknesses:

In-game Adjustments & Effects

General Comments

Left Sides	Left Sides
Right Side(s)/Opposite	Right Side(s)/Opposite
Setter(s)	Setter(s)
Middles	Middles
Libero	Libero

Player(s) of the Match

Moment of the Match

Final Analysis

Notes

Match Analysis II

Team #1__________________

Wins: ___ Losses: ___

Date: ______________________

Team #2_____________________

Wins: ___ Losses: ___

Court: ________________________

Offense/Rotation:

Strengths:

Weaknesses:

Offense/Rotation:

Strengths:

Weaknesses:

In-game Adjustments & Effects

General Comments

Left Sides

Right Side(s)/Opposite

Setter(s)

Middles

Libero

Left Sides

Right Side(s)/Opposite

Setter(s)

Middles

Libero

Player(s) of the Match

Moment of the Match

Final Analysis

Notes

NOTES PAGES

Date______________ Title______________

Date______________ Title______________

Notes

Date______________ Title______________

Date______________ Title______________

Notes

Date______________ Title______________

Date____________ Title____________

Notes

Date______________ Title______________

Date______________ Title______________

Notes

Date______________ Title______________

Date______________ Title______________

Notes

ABOUT THE AUTHORS

Richard Kent

David Gallagher

Richard Kent, Ph.D., is a professor at the University of Maine. A former Olympic Development Program soccer coach and state ski coach, Kent is the author of many books, including *Writing on the Bus: Using Athletic Team Notebooks and Journals to Advance Learning and Performance in Sports*. Kent works with teams, athletes, and coaches across the USA.

David Gallagher, Ph.D., is a professor at Mount Saint Mary College where he teaches courses in adolescent literacy and secondary education methods. A former captain and setter at Boston University and Michigan State University, Gallagher has been in gyms and on sand courts playing volleyball since the age of five.

For more information on athletes' journals and team notebooks, visit
WRITINGATHLETES.COM

Write. Learn. Perform.

Made in the USA
Monee, IL
14 October 2021

80036640R00085